The Further BLURTINGS of
BAXTER

JEDSON WAS NOTED FOR HIS
WITHERING SIDELONG GLANCES

LITTLE, BROWN AND COMPANY
Boston · New York · Toronto · London

A LITTLE, BROWN BOOK

This edition published in Great Britain in 1994 by Little, Brown and Company

Copyright © 1994 by Glen Baxter
The moral right of the author has been asserted

A CIP catalogue record for this book is available from the British Library

ISBN 0-316-90988-2

10 9 8 7 6 5 4 3 2 1

Designed by David Fordham

PRINTED AND BOUND IN ITALY

The majority of the images reproduced in this book are available as greetings cards from Santoro Graphics, 63 Maltings Place, Bagley's Lane, London SW6 2BY

Little, Brown and Company (UK) Ltd
Brettenham House
Lancaster Place
London WC2E 7EN

ERINA TRIES TO BE POPULAR

'YOU KNOW,' said Erina, as she made
a knot in her sock and picked up another tub of lead, 'I think we're all the
most frightful duds here.' The other
six girls raised their legs, put down
their cigars and gazed at her in
astonishment.

'Well, just look at us,' snapped Ruth, as
she rasped her fist on a tub. 'All working
hard to avoid the school bazaar.'

'Well we like doing it,' argued Daphne.

'Yes, it's great fun avoiding things,' agreed Monica.

Erina puckered her forehead as she thought of Joan. It was the day before the
annual storm and all the girls were in a great hurry to wash and shave. The
thought of Joan made shaving easier.

'I could almost learn to steal jewellery,' mused Erina, raising her foot to
describe a lazy semicircle in the air just below Monica's chin.

'But we haven't any to steal,' interrupted Joan.

'I could forge notes, bully new girls and steal shaving kits,'
noted Erina.

'But why should you?' queried Ruth.

'Because that's how to start a career,' stated Erina slowly.

'What are you all going on about?' asked Daphne. 'I
thought we were all supposed to be concentrating on height-
ening awareness.'

'You're none of you truly serious,' cried Erina. 'You see,
I've decided not to listen to advice any more. I'm going to be a maniac.'

'Thanks awfully,' said Monica. 'That's the first interesting thing I've heard
you utter.'

The girls were not particularly surprised when Erina spoke. For the whole of
the first term she had been busy deciding on new careers and already she had

ERINA SET ASIDE AN HOUR
EACH DAY TO WORK ON HER
THREATENING LETTERS

been an explorer, scientist and docker. For three whole weeks she had been polishing boulders.

'It's true,' snorted Erina in triumph. 'I shave my head tonight.'

At the stroke of nine Erina appeared, her head freshly shaved.

'What a head,' exclaimed Philippa smartly. 'It's like a heap of pock-marked gravel.'

Erina did not speak. She was staring at the tall figure marching towards her down the corridor.

'She's using her feet,' observed Ruth tartly.

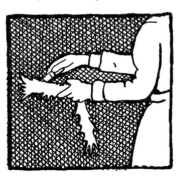

'Shut up,' snapped Daphne, poking idly at her snood.

'Hush,' squeaked Joan, 'she's Lady Warren and she knows absolutely nothing.'

The girls rose to their feet as she approached.

'Don't let me disturb you,' announced the visitor. 'I understand you've all been shaving again.'

She stopped for several minutes to admire Erina's baldness, Monica's lavender bags and the smooth muscles of an indifferent Ruth. They were the most stunning muscles she had ever seen. They glistened occasionally. 'I certainly must tell my friends about these,' hissed Lady Warren. 'Could you allow me a tweak?'

Erina stood by, glowering. The very next thing she did was to find the school matron and ask if she might set fire to the sanatorium.

'Certainly not,' snapped matron firmly, 'I have never heard of such an idea. Besides, I have a headache.'

Erina sighed as she trudged slowly back to the dormitory. She decided that it was not at all easy to be a maniac.

GLEN BAXTER 1994

WE ADVISED HIM AS TO WHERE
HE MIGHT PLACE HIS HERRING

"I HAVE TO INFORM YOU THAT UP HERE IN 261^B WE TEND TO FAVOUR THE SPOON WHEN TACKLING MINESTRONE" GROWLED TEX

ONLY THE DISTANT THUD OF QUICHE
UPON CONCRETE SUGGESTED TO FRANK
THAT SPRING WAS ALMOST HERE

THE INSURANCE SALESMAN MOVED
IN BRANDISHING HIS POLICIES

SLOWLY, BUT WITH UNERRING PRECISION,
DR. TUTTLE REACHED FOR HIS LUGER

"HOME EARLY FROM THE OFFICE AGAIN, DEAR?" SNAPPED IRMA

"WE'LL HAVE NO ALLITERATION IN THIS HERE BUNKHOUSE" SNORTED McCULLOCH

YOUNG ARTHUR'S EARRINGS WERE
THE TALK OF NOTTINGHAM

ROBIN WAS CERTAINLY IMPRESSED
WITH THE SIMULATED TEAK FINISH

I KNEW IT WAS AN OUTSIDE CHANCE, BUT IF I COULD KEEP THE ANTS IN LINE, WE MIGHT JUST REACH CAMP MORESBY BEFORE DAWN...

WITH THE ARRIVAL OF SPRING
DR. SCHREIBER RESUMED HIS
WORK ON THE ERADICATION
OF THE COMMON GREENFLY

IT WAS THE WORST CASE OF
DANDRUFF THEY HAD EVER SEEN

THE HOLIDAY BEGAN WITH
ANOTHER PETTY FAMILY SQUABBLE

MR BECKER ALWAYS LAID ON A
SPECIAL WELCOME FOR THE LADS

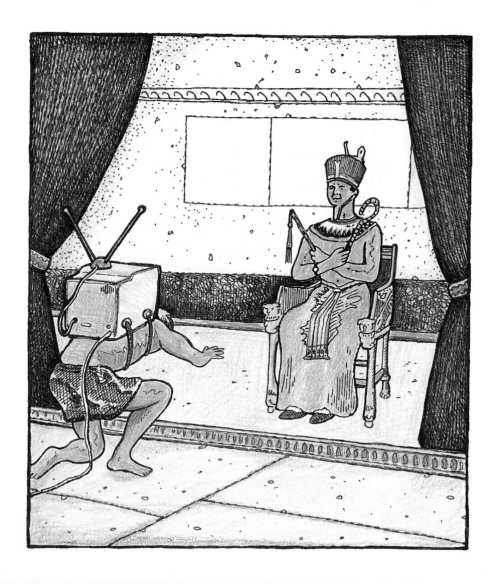

IT WAS DIFFICULT TO ARGUE WITH A MAN WHOSE KNOWLEDGE OF THE EARLY RECORDINGS OF CONNIE FRANCIS WAS PRACTICALLY FLAWLESS

OLD CATTERMOLE WAS OUT IN
THE GARDEN TENDING THE FUCHSIAS

SECURING BREAKFAST WAS PROVING
TO BE SOMEWHAT MORE DIFFICULT
THAN I HAD AT FIRST IMAGINED

ALTHOUGH THERE SEEMED TO BE A GENERAL LACK OF AMENITIES, I WAS FORTUNATE ENOUGH TO HAVE BEEN GIVEN MY OWN BED

LUCKILY WE HAD BEEN ABLE TO
FIND A PARKING SPOT WITHIN
EASY REACH OF THE CITY CENTRE

OUR VILLA WAS ACTUALLY
A FEW INCHES LARGER
THAN THE PHOTOGRAPH
IN THE BROCHURE

MANY WERE THE OCCASIONS WHEN I CHOSE NOT TO PARTICIPATE IN THOSE EARNEST AFTER-DINNER DEBATES

I LIKED TO THINK THAT OURS WAS A RATHER SPECIAL RELATIONSHIP

I WAS STILL NOT ENTIRELY
HAPPY WITH THE SLEEPING
ARRANGEMENTS

"IF THERE HAS BEEN A MISHAP ON THE SPORTS FIELD, THEN QUITE NATURALLY I WOULD LIKE TO BE THE FIRST TO BE INFORMED" MUMBLED THE HEADMASTER

"I'M AFRAID WHAT THIS MEANS, YOUNG JIMMY, IS THAT TECHNICALLY, YOU'RE A GONER"

JANET HAD OPTED TO FLY
"TOURIST CLASS"

"SO JUST EXACTLY WHAT IS THIS REVOLUTIONARY BREAKTHROUGH IN FURNITURE DESIGN OF YOURS, EH?" SNAPPED THE IMPATIENT LUCY.

AS A JUGGLER OF THE SINGLE
ORANGE, HE WAS QUITE CLEARLY
AN ACKNOWLEDGED MASTER

IT SOON BECAME APPARENT
THAT BRENDA WOULD NOT BE
SHARING HER MEATBALL WITH
THE REST OF US AFTER ALL

"I THINK YOU KNOW WHY I'VE CHOSEN YOU FOR THE JOB, ARKRIGHT" WHISPERED EDNA